AUGUSTA READ THOMAS

TOFT SERENADE

FOR VIOLIN AND PIANO

ED 4493
First Printing: September 2011

ISBN 978-1-4584-1391-8

G. SCHIRMER, *Inc.*

DISTRIBUTED BY

HAL•LEONARD®
CORPORATION
7777 W. BLUEMOUND RD. P.O. BOX 13819 MILWAUKEE, WI 53213

www.schirmer.com
www.halleonard.com

"Toft Serenade" for violin and piano (2006) was commissioned by
Christopher and Douglas Toft for their parents, Richard and Marietta,
in honor of their respective 70th and 65th birthdays.

It was premiered by Rachel Barton Pine, violin and Matthew Hagle, piano
in Chicago on 28 October 2006 at a private party.

A version of "Toft Serenade" is available for viola and piano.
It is identical to the violin version, merely transposed down a perfect fifth
and with a few octave changes on the low notes in the piano part.

duration ca. 6 minutes

PROGRAM NOTE:

In two colorful sections, which are played seamlessly, *Toft Serenade* starts with a majestic, lyrical, long solo violin song, as if the violinist was persistently serenading outside of their lover's window at midnight! This tuneful melody is supported by resonant piano harmonies (somewhat reminiscent of a guitar strumming along, accompanying the serenading violinist in an *almost* overtly "*sweet*" manner - on purpose).

The midnight serenade works! In the second section, which is playful, spirited, virtuosic, airborne, and vibrant, imagine that the serenaded climbs out of the window and runs away, forever and ever, with their lover.

This Serenade is organic and, at every level, concerned with transformations and connections. Although this music is highly notated, precise, carefully structured, thoughtfully proportioned, and so forth—and although you have two musicians elegantly working together from the very specific text—I like my music to be played so that the "inner-life" of the different rhythmic syntaxes is specific, with characterized phrasing of the colors and harmonies, etc., keeping it ultra alive and spontaneous sounding, as if the audience is overhearing a "captured improvisation."

For their sublime precision and technical mastery, I deeply thank Rachel Barton Pine and Matthew Hagle for premiering my serenade in this manner.

—Augusta Read Thomas

PERFORMANCE NOTES:

Dynamics: There are only six dynamics used in this score (*pp, p, mp, mf, f, ff*) so that each "level" of volume has a clear meaning and sound.

Piano Pedals: There are places where the piano's damper pedal is held down for long periods of time. These pedal markings are accurate and maximum harmonic resonance is desired. *l.v. (laissez vibrer)* ties are not marked but are implied.

Bowings: All bowings are simply suggestions from the composer and can be changed freely by the player with the exception of the bowings shown below. Please move from double-stops to single notes as smoothly as possible.

⌐ = a very fast, full down-bow.

∨⁺ = a slow to fast, intense up-bow.

⊓ _ _ _ _ ⌐ = a single bow should be used for the duration of the dashed line. Pace the bow to last through the passage.

Pizzicato: All pizzicatti are *l.v. molto.*

Grace-notes: All grace-notes come before the beat.

Fermatas: Their duration should depend on the bowings and on the resonance of the performance space. The pointed fermatas are the shortest of the three fermata types. The square fermatas should be longer than the normal, round-in-shape, fermatas. Please vary the durations of each normal, round-in-shape, fermata such that they do not become predictable. In this way, each performance will be slightly different from one another.

These fermatas are meant to "throw off" the pulse and add to the unpredictability and to the desired "un-square-ness" of the flow. They are often an effort to "write-in" very flexible rubato and to add expressivity.

a tempo: Unless a new tempo is specified, then after each fermata, please return to the previous tempo.

for Marietta and Richard with admiration

TOFT SERENADE
for Violin and Piano

Augusta Read Thomas
(2006)

* "Recitative-like." Violinist should "go with the bow" instead of counting exact rhythms.

** ⋈ = very fast, full down-bow.

*** V⁺ = slow to fast, intense up-bow.

**** Through measure 41, somewhat akin to a strumming guitar, accompanying the serenading violinist; almost overtly saccharine or syrupy.

* Molto rubato and very expressive despite the softer dynamic and harmonic.

** Bowing indications followed by a dashed line indicate a single bow should be used. Pace the bow to last through the passage.

*** It is optional to play the A in measure 22 as a harmonic sul A.

**** It is optional to play some or all the high D's as harmonics.

* One long phrase from the final third of measure 36 through measure 45, which is getting more and more intense and passionate.

** It is optional to play the G in measures 44 and 45 as a harmonic sul G.

*** This measure should be no longer than one beat.

**Playful, like an improvisation,
energized** ♩ = 132

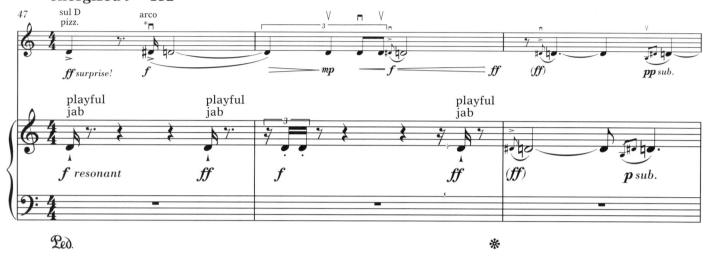

a tempo ♩ = **104–108**

* The loud D's should be played on the open D string while the soft D's should be played on the G string with vibrato.

Augusta Read Thomas

TOFT SERENADE

Violin

PERFORMANCE NOTES

Dynamics: There are only six dynamics used in this score (*pp, p, mp, mf, f, ff*) so that each "level" of volume has a clear meaning and sound.

Piano Pedals: There are places where the piano's damper pedal is held down for long periods of time. These pedal markings are accurate and maximum harmonic resonance is desired. *l.v. (laissez vibrer)* ties are not marked but are implied.

Bowings: All bowings are simply suggestions from the composer and can be changed freely by the player with the exception of the bowings shown below. Please move from double-stops to single notes as smoothly as possible.

⊓ = a very fast, full down-bow.

∨ = a slow to fast, intense up-bow.

⊓_ _ _ _ = a single bow should be used for the duration of the dashed line. Pace the bow to last through the passage.

Pizzicato: All pizzicatti are *l.v. molto*.

Grace-notes: All grace-notes come before the beat.

Fermatas: Their duration should depend on the bowings and on the resonance of the performance space. The pointed fermatas are the shortest of the three fermata types. The square fermatas should be longer than the normal, round-in-shape, fermatas. Please vary the durations of each normal, round-in-shape, fermata such that they do not become predictable. In this way, each performance will be slightly different from one another.

These fermatas are meant to "throw off" the pulse and add to the unpredictability and to the desired "un-square-ness" of the flow. They are often an effort to "write-in" very flexible rubato and to add expressivity.

a tempo: Unless a new tempo is specified, then after each fermata, please return to the previous tempo.

G. SCHIRMER, *Inc.*

DISTRIBUTED BY

HAL•LEONARD®
CORPORATION

7777 W. BLUEMOUND RD. P.O. BOX 13819 MILWAUKEE, WI 53213

TOFT SERENADE
for Violin and Piano

Augusta Read Thomas
(2006)

Violin

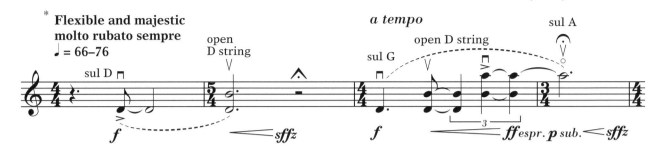

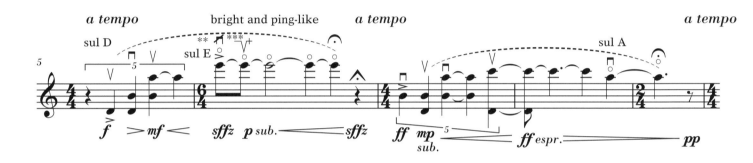

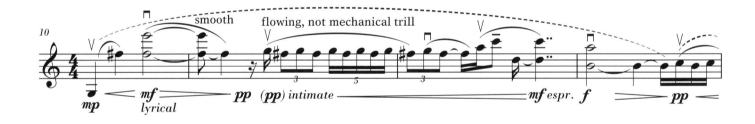

* **"Recitative-like."** Violinist should "go with the bow" instead of counting exact rhythms.

** = very fast, full down-bow.

*** = slow to fast, intense up-bow.

Playful, like an improvisation, energized ♩ = 132

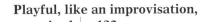

rit.   *a tempo* ♩ = 104–108

rit.

a tempo
♩ = 104–108

(rubato for piano)

Capricious ♩ = 120

long line for next 14 beats

rit.   *a tempo*

* The loud D's should be played on the open D string while the soft D's should be played on the G string with vibrato.

** Optional harmonic sul E.

* Molto rubato and very expressive despite the softer dynamic and harmonic.

** Bowing indications followed by a dashed line indicate a single bow should be used. Pace the bow to last through the passage.

*** It is optional to play the A in measure 22 as a harmonic, sul A.

**** It is optional to play some or all the high D's as harmonics.

***** One long phrase from the final third of measure 36 through measure 45, which is getting more and more intense and passionate.

† It is optional to play the G in measures 44 and 45 as a harmonic sul G.

‡ This measure should be no longer than one beat.

* The held notes of the violin and piano should end at exactly the same moment. The piano pedal should be lifted precisely when violin note ends.

* Optional harmonic, sul E.

6

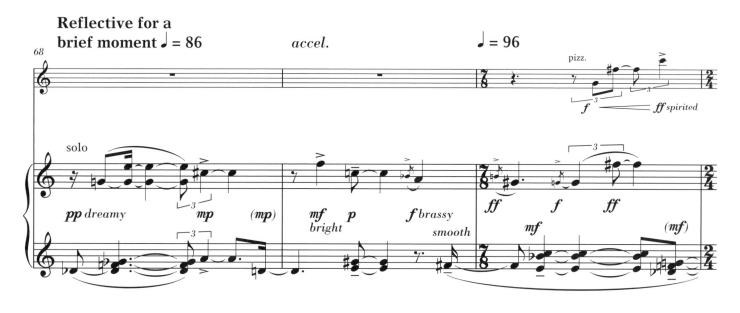

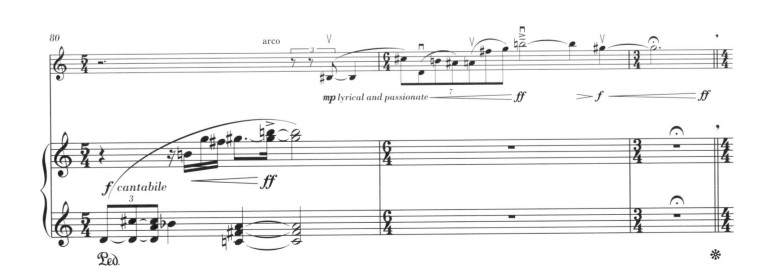

Fiery and colorful,
like a sparkler flickering in all directions
♩ = 104–112

* From here to the end, divide notes between hands.

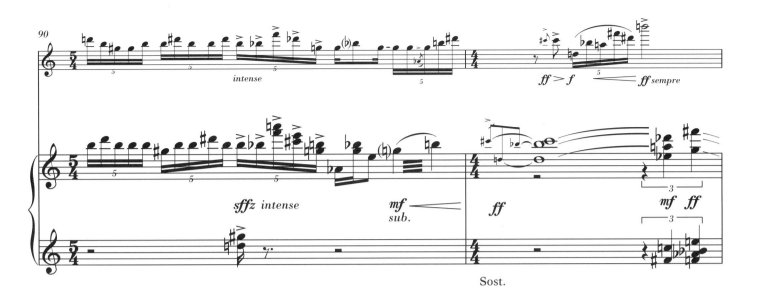

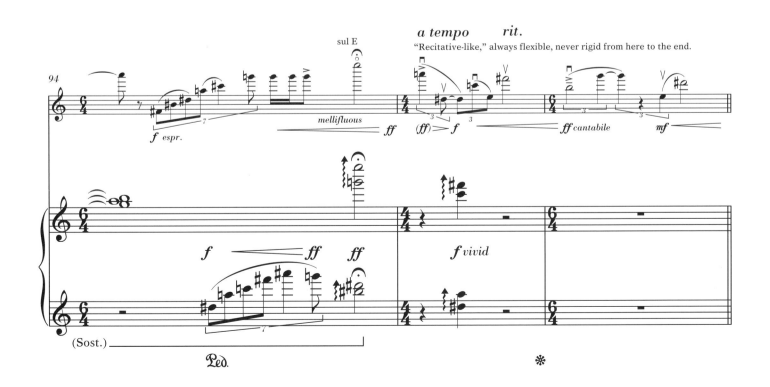

Dramatic and passionate

♩ = 86

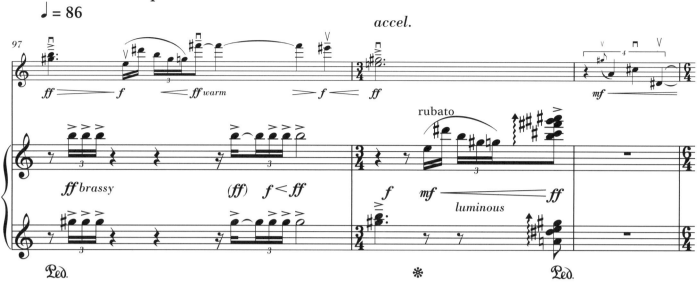

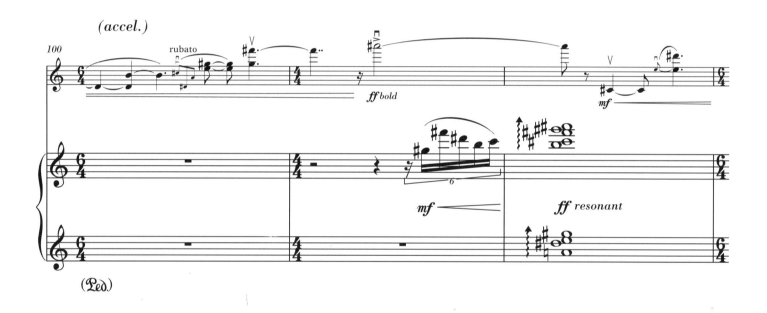

♩ = 98

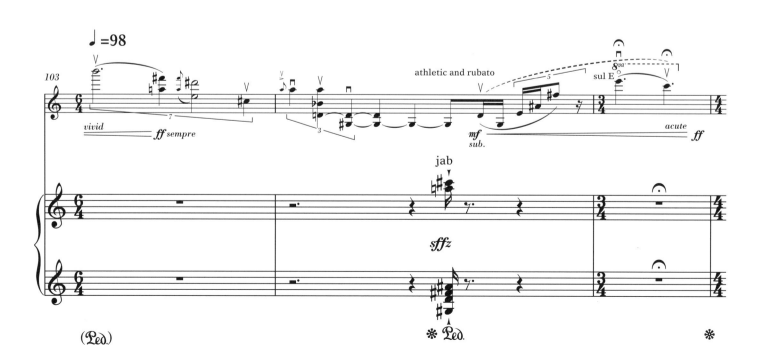

Regal, centered, earthy

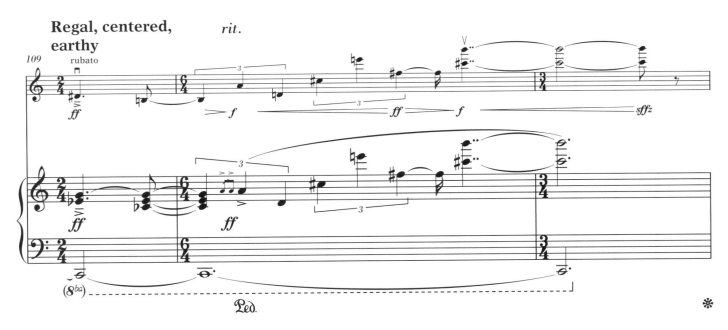

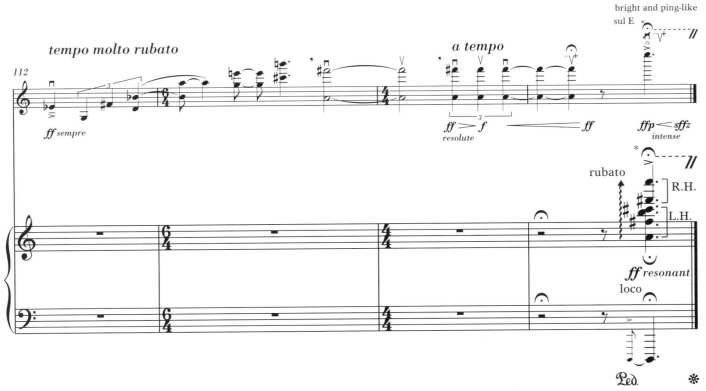

* The held notes should end at exactly the same moment, with the piano pedal lifted precisely when violin note ends.